THE ~~V~~ 20 G~~~~ DEFENDERS

STRIKERS hit the back page headlines for scoring goals that win games. But it's defenders who risk their own limbs with bone-crunching tackles in a bid to stop the opposition from scoring. You'll see them playing in protective head bands, often changing their blood-stained shirts, and have probably watched in horror as these guys have had to be stretchered off, all in the name of keeping a clean sheet. We've trawled the planet to bring you the top keepers, full-backs and central-halves from around the world and it will come as no surprise that many of them grace the English Premiership. You may agree with our Top 20 but there again you may not! You can e-mail comments to Colin Mitchell (colin_mitchell@ipcmedia.com)

PUBLISHED BY

Pedigree®

BOOKS LTD

PEDIGREE BOOKS LTD
BEECH HILL HOUSE
WALNUT GARDENS
ST. DAVIDS HILL
EXETER
DEVON EX4 4DH

books@pedigreegroup.co.uk

Under License from

IPC | INSPIRE
A TimeWarner Company
A part of IPC Media,
a TimeWarner company

™ and © IPC Media Ltd 2008

EDITOR: COLIN MITCHELL **DESIGN & REPRO:** KEITH CHAMBERS **WRITER:** JON REEVES

Use your fantastic free Player Profile Cards to play Fantasy Football! There's the chance to win the Shooty Cup and brilliant prizes!

www.shootycup.co.uk

£6.99

DANIEL
ALVES

DANIEL ALVES

FACTFILE

Full name: Daniel Alves Da Silva
Born: May 6, 1983, Juazeiro, Brazil
Height: 1.71m (5ft 7in)
Weight: 63.9 kg (10st 1lb)
Position: Right-back,
right wing-back
Clubs: EC Bahia and Sevilla

HONOURS

Copa America: 2007
UEFA Cup: 2006, 2007
UEFA Super Cup: 2007
Spanish Copa Del Ray: 2007

DID YOU KNOW?

● Alves scored his first goal for Brazil against Argentina in the final of the 2007 Copa America.
● As well as Chelsea, Liverpool have also been linked with a move for Sevilla's prized asset.

PROFILE

AFTER YEARS AS his country's number one attacking right-back, AC Milan and Brazil legend Cafu, can relax knowing that his country finally has a replacement. Daniel Alves is probably the most skilful and exciting defender in the world at this very moment.

His silky South American skills, frightening pace and ability to score spectacular goals ensure that he stands out as one of Sevilla's danger men. He bombs forward with great enthusiasm, always eager to join the attack and deliver quality into the box. With all these impressive talents it's easy to forget that Alves is in fact a defender!

The full-back position has developed hugely in the modern era and Daniel is the embodiment of the complete right wing-back. In full flow he is almost unplayable, gliding past wingers and defenders, capitalising on his great speed and balance, and providing the team with an extra dimension.

Now a regular in the Brazil squad, the Sevilla star's profile should continue to rise and a move to one of Europe's biggest clubs can't be far away. Chelsea made a couple of bids in the last transfer window and unless Sevilla can really compete in the Champions League, the Brazilian could well be on his way next summer.

WHAT HE SAYS

"Sevilla should look after me. In the four years I have been there, I've given my best. I just want them to listen – my only consideration is to leave the club on good terms. We've been looking at Chelsea's offer for a while and that's the one that interests me."

SHOOTY SAYS:

This kid is a bit special and destined to play for one of Europe's biggest clubs before too long. Dan the man is probably the best wing-back on the planet!

GIANLUIGI BUFFON

FACTFILE

Full name: Gianluigi Buffon
Born: January 28, 1978,
Carrara, Italy
Height: 1.91m (6ft 3in)
Weight: 83kg (13st 1lb)
Position: Goalkeeper
Clubs: Parma and Juventus

HONOURS

World Cup: 2006
UEFA Cup: 1999
Italian Serie A: 2002, 2003, 2005, 2006
(both latter titles stripped due to corruption
and financial irregularities involving Juventus)
Coppa Italia: 1999

DID YOU KNOW?

● The £33m Juventus paid Parma for Buffon's
services in 2001 remains a world record fee
for a goalkeeper.
● Gigi made his Serie A debut for Parma
against AC Milan as a 17-year-old.

PROFILE

THE MOST TALENTED goalkeeper of his generation
and one of the most naturally gifted Italian stoppers
of all time. His agility, speed off his line and great
judgement, complemented by an awesome physical
stature and some super human
reactions, have established
Buffon's reputation as one of
the world's best shot-stoppers.

Gigi forms quite a presence in
goal and has enough big match
practice and experience of dealing
with highly pressurised situations
to allow him to cruise through
games. Excellent distribution,
both from his hands and his feet,
he also casts an intimidating
shadow on the goal-line for any
player taking a penalty – just ask
France's David Trezeguet who
missed his crucial kick against
Gianluigi in the 2006 World Cup Final. Stayed loyal
to Juventus following their demotion to Serie B, and
could taste more success with Italy in the future.

WHAT HE SAYS

"Every time I start playing I really
don't know what will happen,
especially because my position as a goalkeeper
is very much about observing, waiting and
then reacting at the right moment. No matter
how much I practise, I am unable to control
the whole situation and I really enjoy this
uncertainty."

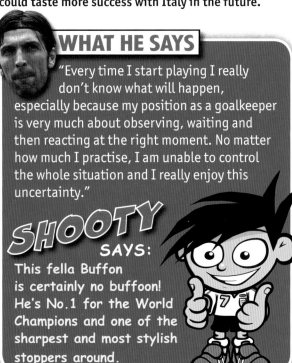

SHOOTY SAYS:

This fella Buffon
is certainly no buffoon!
He's No.1 for the World
Champions and one of the
sharpest and most stylish
stoppers around.

GIANLUIGI BUFFON

FABIO
CANNAVARO

FABIO CANNAVARO

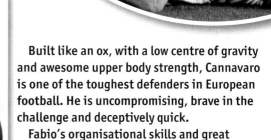

FACTFILE

Full name: Fabio Cannavaro
Born: September 13, 1973,
Naples, Italy
Height: 1.75m (5ft 9in)
Weight: 73.5kg (11st 8lb)
Position: Central-defender
Clubs: Napoli, Parma, Inter Milan,
Juventus and Real Madrid

HONOURS

World Cup: 2006
UEFA Cup: 1999
Serie A: 2005, 2006 (both titles
stripped due to corruption and
financial irregularities involving
Juventus).
La Liga: 2007
Coppa Italia: 1999, 2002
**European Footballer
of the Year:** 2006
FIFA World Player of the Year: 2006
World Soccer **Player of the Year:** 2006

DID YOU KNOW?

● At Madrid, Fabio wears the number five shirt
previously worn by Real legend Zinedine Zidane.
● Fabio's younger brother Paolo is also a defender
and plays for Italian side Napoli.

PROFILE

ITALY'S INSPIRATIONAL CAPTAIN has always been
regarded as one of the world's finest defenders.
In 2006, the centre-back guided Italy to their first
World Cup title since 1982 by marshalling the back
line and inspiring those around him. Cannavaro was
also named World and European Player of the Year.

Fabio has played most of his club football in Italy,
representing his sides with great distinction. He
joined Real Madrid following the World Cup and
helped them to the league title in his first season.

Built like an ox, with a low centre of gravity
and awesome upper body strength, Cannavaro
is one of the toughest defenders in European
football. He is uncompromising, brave in the
challenge and deceptively quick.

Fabio's organisational skills and great
leadership make him Italy's talisman and
his vast experience and big match know-
how will be vital at Euro 2008.

WHAT HE SAYS

"Real Madrid is a very big club and
everything is perfect. Everything is
cured in the minimum details, they are used
to dealing with great players and it shows.
The structure is exceptional and it's an ideal
environment to work in."

SHOOTY SAYS:

Action man look-a-like
Cannavaro is one of
the game's best all-round
defenders. When the going
gets tough, Fabio gets going!
Experienced, but certainly
not pasta his besta!

JAMIE CARRAGHER

FACTFILE

Full name: James Lee Duncan Carragher
Born: January 28, 1978, Bootle, Liverpool
Height: 1.85m (6ft 1in)
Weight: 76kg (12st)
Position: Central-defender
Clubs: Liverpool

HONOURS

UEFA Champions League: 2005
UEFA Cup: 2001
FA Cup: 2001, 2006
League Cup: 2001, 2003
European Super Cup: 2001, 2005

DID YOU KNOW?

● Jamie was part of Liverpool's 1996 FA Youth Cup-winning team, along with Michael Owen.
● He has been awarded the freedom of the Borough of Sefton due to his vast amount of work for local charities.

PROFILE

LIVERPOOL FANS SING a song about their dream of a team of Carraghers, and when you see the passion and commitment that Jamie shows for the Reds' cause, it's easy to see why. Carra plays every game like it could be his last and the tough-tackler is always up for a battle, although he is a great reader of the game.

It took Jamie a few seasons to establish himself as a first-team regular, often playing in midfield or at full-back, but following Rafa Benitez's arrival at Anfield, he has cemented his status as a top centre-back.

Carra was a hero during Liverpool's 2005 Champions League victory as he threw himself into blocks and tackles, despite limping around with cramp in extra-time.

Retired from England duty in 2007 after repeatedly being overlooked for a starting place. Known as "probably the best Scouser in the world".

WHAT HE SAYS

"This is the best club in the world with the best fans, and I'm very proud to be a Liverpool player. I never really played centre-half for England and, to be honest, I've never really played that well for them as I played a lot of the time at full-back."

SHOOTY SAYS:

Jamie Carragher is one of the best things to come out of Liverpool since The Beatles! Committed, a crowd pleaser, class... Carragher.

JAMIE
CARRAGHER

RICARDO CARVALHO

RICARDO CARVALHO

FACTFILE

Full name: Ricardo Alberto Silveira Carvalho
Born: May 18, 1978, Amarante, Portugal
Height: 1.83m (6ft)
Weight: 79.8kg (12st 8lb)
Position: Central-defender
Clubs: FC Porto, Vitoria FC (loan), FC Alverca (loan) and Chelsea

HONOURS

UEFA Champions League: 2004
UEFA Cup: 2003
Premier League:
2005, 2006
Portuguese Superliga:
2003, 2004
FA Cup: 2007
League Cup: 2005, 2007
Portuguese Player of the Year: 2003

A regular in the Portugal side, where he forms an impressive partnership with Fernando Meira, Ricardo impressed at Euro 2004 and the 2006 World Cup.

Now one of Chelsea's most influential performers and the Blues just don't look the same side without either him or John Terry in the centre of defence.

DID YOU KNOW?

● When they snapped up Carvalho from FC Porto in 2004, Chelsea paid the Portuguese side a whopping £19.85m for his services.
● Ricardo was at the centre of the World Cup 2006 quarter-final row, when Wayne Rooney was sent off for allegedly stamping on him – and Cristiano Ronaldo performed his infamous wink.

PROFILE

RICARDO CARVALHO HAS has proved himself as one of the finest defenders in Europe since joining Chelsea from Porto in 2005. He is a classic European-style stopper who can and will use any means necessary to prevent an attacker gaining an advantage.

Awkward, aggressive and strong in the air, Ricardo is perfectly suited to the battles of the Premiership, but also has class and ability on the ball. Often starts Chelsea attacks with a clever pass or through ball.

WHAT HE SAYS

"All I think about is how to improve as a player. Some players will play nine or ten years at the top level and will still never win the Champions League. But if I can win it for a second time – this time with Chelsea – it will be absolutely fantastic."

SHOOTY SAYS:

Ricardo can 'carve' up even the best centre-forwards with his awesome power in the tackle and his strength in the air. A proper Portuguese man-of-war!

IKER CASILLAS

FACTFILE

Full name: Iker Casillas Fernandez
Born: May 20, 1981, Madrid, Spain
Height: 1.85m (6ft 1in)
Weight: 78.5kg (12st 5lb)
Position: Goalkeeper
Clubs: Real Madrid

HONOURS

UEFA Champions League: 2000, 2002
Spanish La Liga: 2001, 2003, 2007
European Super Cup: 2002
Intercontinental Cup: 2002

DID YOU KNOW?

● Iker was born on the same day as Chelsea stopper Petr Cech, but he is a year older.
● He became the youngest-ever goalkeeper to play in a European Cup Final when he represented Real Madrid in the 2000 showpiece.

PROFILE

IT'S AMAZING THAT Iker Casillas is still only 26-years-old, as he seems to have been around forever. The Spain stopper broke into the Real Madrid first-team as a teenager and has been the first choice for club and country ever since.

Showing great composure, razor sharp reflexes, a chess player's concentration and a big match temperament well beyond his years, Iker burst onto the European scene in 2000.

Famed for his ability to command his area, his sharpness to close down forwards and some spectacular saves, the Spain No.1 has been one of Madrid's most consistent performers, despite having to play in front of some far from watertight defences.

He has seen Zidane, Beckham and Figo move on, played under many managers, won the Champions League twice and already played in a World Cup.

WHAT HE SAYS

"I was very lucky to be able to start at a very young age and things have turned out well. I arrived here at the age of eight and I am still part of the set-up and still love it. I have won many titles, had some wonderful experiences and I can't see myself anywhere else. I'll be staying put."

SHOOTY SAYS:

Iker has collected more bling than Kanye West keeps in one of his mansions! Spain's number one is a super stopper.

IKER
CASILLAS

PETR CECH

PETR CECH

DID YOU KNOW?

● Petr holds the record for most clean sheets in a Premiership season thanks to the 25 shut-outs he and Chelsea maintained during the 2004-05 title-winning campaign.
● The sickening injury Cech suffered after his collision with Reading's Stephen Hunt needed 30 stitches and led to him wearing head gear.

PROFILE

THE GIANT CZECH stopper is arguably the best goalkeeper on the planet right now, and is certainly the Premiership's number one. His imposing frame, ability to command his area and great technical ability, combined with awesome reflexes and sound distribution, ensure he possesses all the qualities a top keeper requires.

The Chelsea man also shows great consistency and experience beyond his years. Still only 25, which for a goalkeeper is just past nappy wearing age, Petr should be one of the world's finest shot-stoppers for many years to come.

His awesome record in the Premiership proves that he can earn Chelsea at least ten points a season. His importance to the team was highlighted last season when he missed most of the campaign due to a serious head injury received against Reading and the Blues' form seriously suffered as a result.

Cech has since returned and is firmly back to his best, wearing his distinctive head guard and still showing remarkable ability.

WHAT HE SAYS

"I spent 100 days, coming in at nine, not leaving until five, working, working, working. I did everything I was told to do and gave it 100 per cent. I've got used to playing with head gear so I don't really feel any difference. It's like in ice hockey, all the players were helmets."

SHOOTY SAYS:

Petr is the Premiership's number one top stopper and all strikers know it's Cech mate when he's bearing down on them! A true Blues' hero!

ASHLEY COLE

final tie against Portugal, the tournament's hosts.

Made his mark at Arsenal where Arsene Wenger gave him the licence to bomb forward and join the attack, often creating goals for the likes of Thierry Henry and Robert Pires.

Ashley revelled in the attacking role as his natural pace, fitness and skill meant he was almost playing as a wing-back in a 4-4-2.

Since joining Chelsea, he has got forward less, but has improved his defending, and as his understanding with Joe Cole develops on the left, both for Chelsea and England, he will soon offer more of an attacking threat.

FACTFILE

Full name: Ashley Cole
Born: December 20, 1980, Stepney, London
Height: 1.71m (5ft 7in)
Weight: 67.1kg (10st 8lb)
Position: Left-back
Clubs: Arsenal, Crystal Palace (loan) and Chelsea

HONOURS

Premier League: 2002, 2004
FA Cup: 2002, 2003, 2005, 2007
League Cup: 2007

DID YOU KNOW?

● Ashley started his career as a striker and made his Arsenal debut as a forward, until Arsene Wenger converted him into an attacking left-back.

● He is married to Girls Aloud singer Cheryl Cole, formerly Tweedy.

PROFILE

ENGLAND'S FIRST CHOICE left-back has proved himself as one of Europe's best in his position. Ashley really came to prominence playing for England at Euro 2004, where he was voted the best left-back in the finals and had the explosive Cristiano Ronaldo firmly in his pocket for most of the Three Lions' quarter-

WHAT HE SAYS

"Coming from a rival club, you are always going to have doubters thinking you are here for certain reasons. But I can definitely say that I am here [at Chelsea] for good reasons – to win things. I have always been a winner and I always will be."

SHOOTY SAYS:

Arguably England's best left-back since Stuart 'Psycho' Pearce, Chelsea star Ash Cole really is hot stuff!

ASHLEY COLE

RIO
FERDINAND

RIO FERDINAND

FACTFILE

Full name: Rio Gavin Ferdinand
Born: November 7, 1978,
Peckham, London
Height: 1.88m (6ft 2in)
Weight: 79.4kg (12st 7lb)
Position: Central-defender
Clubs: West Ham United,
Bournemouth (loan), Leeds
United and Manchester United

HONOURS

Premier League:
2003, 2007
League Cup: 2006

DID YOU KNOW?

● Rio was named in the 2006-07
PFA Premiership Team of the
Season alongside seven United team-mates.
● His brother is West Ham defender Anton and his
cousin is former QPR, Newcastle, Tottenham and
England striker Les Ferdinand... who also played
for the Hammers late in his career!

PROFILE

IF JOHN TERRY is England's rock at the back, then
Rio Ferdinand is the Three Lions' Rolls Royce. The
Man United star has been one of the Red Devils'
most consistent performers since his English
record £30m transfer from Leeds in 2002.

His amazing composure and ability on the ball,
coupled with his awesome physical attributes and
a natural reading of the game, make Rio one of the
finest defenders around. His range of passing is better
than most midfielders. When he brings the ball out
from defence he causes all kinds of problems and is
comfortable dribbling past players.

In recent seasons he has formed an excellent
defensive partnership at United with Nemanja Vidic,
as the Serb's aggression and classic defenders'
qualities have provided the perfect
blend for Ferdinand's classy, more
sweeper-like style.

At major tournaments, such as
the 2002 and 2006 World Cups, Rio
has managed to raise his game even
further and proved himself to be one
of the best defenders on the planet.

WHAT HE SAYS

"I think the money in football today
is crazy. But I'm just fortunate and
blessed I'm in this industry and I thank God
every morning that I wake up that I can do
work and a job that I actually enjoy."

SHOOTY

SAYS:
One of the coolest
defenders there is
and probably England's
most talented centre-
back since the great Bobby
Moore. Rio rocks!

WILLIAM GALLAS

FACTFILE

Full name: William Gallas
Born: August 17, 1977,
Asnieres-sur-Seine, France
Height: 1.8m (5ft 11in)
Weight: 72.1kg (11st 5lb)
Position: Central-defender,
full-back
Clubs: Caen, Olympique Marseille, Chelsea and Arsenal

HONOURS

Premier League: 2005, 2006
League Cup: 2005

DID YOU KNOW?

● Despite being a defender, William actually wears the No.10 shirt for Arsenal. It was previously worn by Gunners' legend Dennis Bergkamp.
● The match-fixing scandal that rocked Italian football ruined his hopes of playing for Juventus or AC Milan, who had both expressed an interest in the player. Instead, Chelsea gave Arsenal Gallas, plus £5m, in exchange for Ashley Cole.

PROFILE

WHEN ARSENAL TRADED Ashley Cole for William Gallas in 2006 they got an excellent deal. Sure, they lost one of the finest attacking left-backs in European football, but they gained arguably one of the most capable defenders to have played in the Premiership in recent years.

When fit, William is a regular for France, and was part of the 2003 Confederations Cup-winning side and the team that reached the 2006 World Cup Final, where they lost to Italy in a penalty shoot-out.

After arriving in England from Marseille in 2001, Gallas soon showed his defensive class at Chelsea, with lightning pace, brute strength and great reading of the game to break up attacks. Also gets forward to good effect.

A danger from set-pieces thanks to an awesome leap and his aggressive predatory instinct in the penalty area, Gallas suffered injuries after his move across London, but once he gets a run in the side, Arsenal fans will love him.

WHAT HE SAYS

"When Italians feel they're being dominated they try to provoke you. They are cheaters, but we can't stop that. I was firm about my wanting to leave Chelsea and I will explain in due time why I wanted to."

SHOOTY SAYS:

Gallas is a top defender and has plenty of space in his back pocket for even the most dangerous strikers. Watch out, Billy boy's gonna get ya!

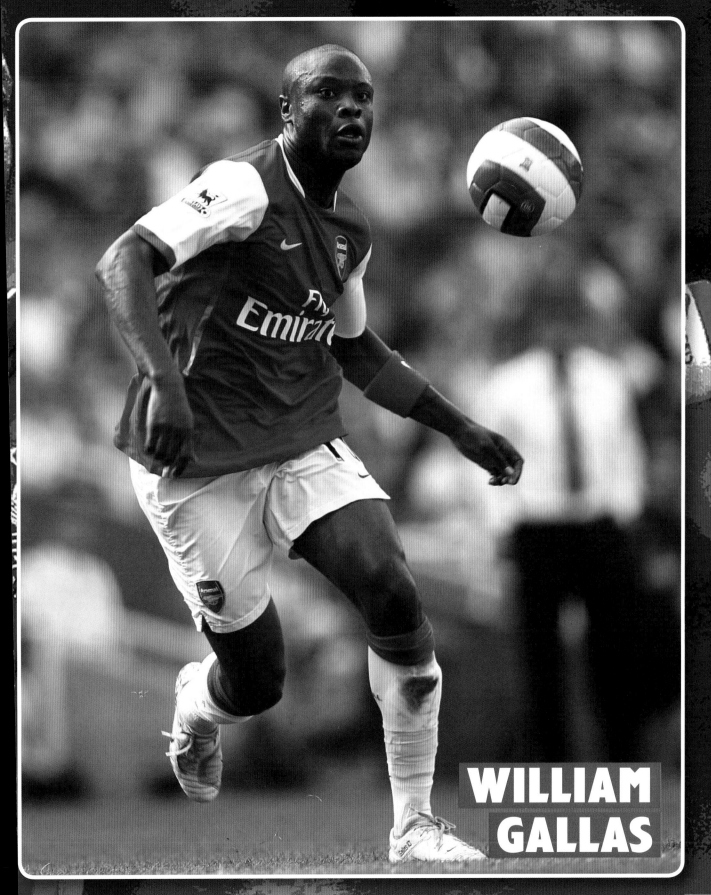

WILLIAM GALLAS

MAREK
JANKULOVSKI

MAREK JANKULOVSKI

FACTFILE

Full name: Marek Jankulovski
Born: May 9, 1977,
Ostrava, Czech Republic
Height: 1.85m (6ft 1in)
Weight: 80.3kg (12st 9lb)
Position: Full-back,
wing-back, midfielder
Clubs: Banik Ostrava,
Napoli, Udinese and AC Milan

HONOURS

UEFA Champions League: 2007
European Super Cup: 2007

DID YOU KNOW?

● Marek has been a regular in the Czech Republic side for seven years and earned over 50 caps.
● A genuine utility man, Marek has played as a winger and a striker during his club career.

PROFILE

VERSATILE AND DEPENDABLE, Czech ace Marek Jankulovski is one of the most solid defenders in the Italian top-flight. His displays for AC Milan and the Czech Republic have been of the highest quality.

Whether playing as a full-back, central-defender or in midfield, Marek's work-rate, ability to read the game and competitive nature make him hard to play against. An excellent man-marker, strong in the tackle and composed on the ball, he starred during Euro 2004 when his impressive displays were vital as the Czech Republic progressed to the semis.

A Champions League winner with Milan, Marek should remain a vital cog in the Rossineri's defence in future seasons.

WHAT HE SAYS

"I'm at Milan, my dream has come true. I play on the left flank, in my national team in defence and while at Udinese I was in midfield. Here at Milan it will be up to Carlo Ancelotti to decide."

SHOOTY SAYS:

This tough Czech defender would tackle his own grandma if she got in the way. Marek is top drawer!

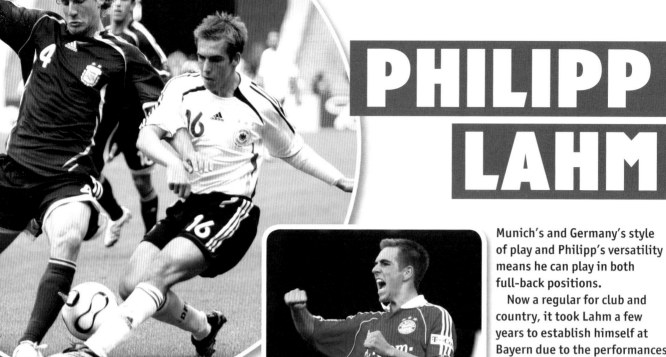

PHILIPP LAHM

FACTFILE

Full name: Philipp Lahm
Born: November 11, 1983, Munich, Germany
Height: 1.71m (5ft 7in)
Weight: 63.9kg (10st 1lb)
Position: Left-back
Clubs: Bayern Munich and VfB Stuttgart (loan)

HONOURS

German Bundesliga: 2003, 2006
German Cup: 2003, 2006

DID YOU KNOW?

● Philipp scored the opening goal of the 2006 World Cup when his long range curler put the Germans 1-0 up against Costa Rica in the sixth minute of the first game.
● He was the only player to play every minute of Germany's World Cup campaign on home soil.

PROFILE

DIMINUTIVE, DEPENDABLE AND dangerous going forward, Philipp Lahm is one of the finest all-round full-backs in European football. His awesome pace, low centre of gravity and deceptive strength enable him to challenge attackers and get forward. His lung-busting runs down the flanks are vital to Bayern Munich's and Germany's style of play and Philipp's versatility means he can play in both full-back positions.

Now a regular for club and country, it took Lahm a few years to establish himself at Bayern due to the performances of experienced France full-backs Bixente Lizarazu and Willy Sagnol.

He was sent on loan to VfB Stuttgart, where his potential transformed into consistent performances, and Munich called him back to make him a first-team regular.

Still only 24, the right-footed left-back has a big future and will be vital to Germany's hopes of success at Euro 2008.

WHAT HE SAYS

"It is true, my right foot is stronger than the left. But I have played 11 years at FC Bayern, and since then it is clear that I've worked on it. It remains an obstacle, but is all in order."

SHOOTY **SAYS:**
This lad is dynamite when he gets going! He can tackle, pass, dribble and shoot – not bad for a defender! Lahm is definitely not lame.

PHILIPP
LAHM

CHRISTOPH
METZELDER

CHRISTOPH METZELDER

FACTFILE

Full name: Christoph Metzelder
Born: November 5, 1980,
Haltern, Germany
Height: 1.93m (6ft 4in)
Weight: 83kg (13st 1lb)
Position: Central-defender
Clubs: Preuben Munster, Borussia
Dortmund and Real Madrid

HONOURS

Bundesliga: 2002
Best Young Player in Europe: 2002

DID YOU KNOW?

● Christoph's younger brother Jan
Malte was on the books at German
club Borussia Dortmund as a
teenager and now plays for lower
league club FC Ingolstadt 04.
● He played in the 2002 World Cup Final
for Germany aged just 21.

PROFILE

THE RELIABLE GERMAN defender is beginning
to show just why he's rated by many as the most
promising centre-back in Europe. With his imposing
physical frame, the lanky Real Madrid star towers
over most strikers and is as hard to beat on the
ground as he is in the air.

Metzelder came to the fore during the 2006 World
Cup when, alongside Per Mertesacker, he formed a
solid back-line which allowed Jurgen
Klinsmann's side to play their attacking,
flowing football.

After impressing at international level
and with Borussia Dortmund, he was
snapped up by Real Madrid in summer
2007 and began to look the real deal as
he adapted to the faster style of play and
improved his touch and range of passing.

WHAT HE SAYS

"I feel something very special for being
part of the best club in the world.
I feel positive arrogance for this, like the one
felt by Bayern Munich players in Germany. Many
Spaniards revere the club and the rest
possibly hate it, but they all
respect it."

SHOOTY SAYS:

A defender's defender,
the German centre-back
doesn't take any prisoners.
Metzelder is da man!

ALLESANDRO NESTA

The AC Milan man is one of the silkiest centre-backs in European football and reads the game brilliantly. He is an excellent man-marker but can drop deep to play more like a sweeper, intercepting passes and tidying up any sloppy play by his team-mates or opponents.

He's no slouch chasing down players and has the height and strength to deal with crosses into the box. When tackling, his timing is impeccable, and his distribution is excellent.

Missed Italy's 2006 World Cup success through injury, and has since announced his international retirement. With Fabio Cannavaro, he formed one of the most impressive defensive partnerships in the modern game.

FACTFILE

Full name: Allesandro Nesta
Born: March 19, 1976, Rome, Italy
Height: 1.83m (6ft)
Weight: 78kg (12st 4lb)
Position: Central-defender
Clubs: Lazio and AC Milan

HONOURS

World Cup: 2006
UEFA Champions League: 2003, 2007
Serie A: 2000, 2004
Coppa Italia: 1998, 2000, 2003
UEFA Cup Winners Cup: 1999
UEFA Super Cup: 1999, 2003, 2007

DID YOU KNOW?

● Allesandro was a member of the Italy squad that won the 1996 UEFA European Under-21 Championship. He was also named top defender in the competition.
● On July 20, 2007, he ended his international career, because of fatigue and recurrent injuries.

PROFILE

WHEN YOU THINK of Italian defenders you think of tough, uncompromising man-markers who grab handfuls of their opponents' shirts and regularly obstruct players, but Nesta is slightly different.

WHAT HE SAYS

"The worst experience I ever had was playing against Ronaldo when we faced Internazionale in the 1998 UEFA Cup Final in Paris. He's an incredible player. I have watched that game on video so many times since then, trying to work out what I did wrong. We lost 3-0 but I don't think now it was my fault. Ronaldo was simply unstoppable."

SHOOTY SAYS:

Despite Allesandro having hair like your Mum, we take our hats off to the AC Milan star. Nesta is one of the besta!

ALLESANDRO
NESTA

CARLES PUYOL

CARLES PUYOL

FACTFILE

Full name: Carles Puyol i Saforcada
Born: April 13, 1978,
La Pobla de Segur, Spain
Height: 1.78m (5ft 10in)
Weight: 78.9kg (12st 6lb)
Position: Central-defender
Clubs: Barcelona

HONOURS

UEFA Champions League: 2006
La Liga: 2005, 2006
UEFA Champions League Defender of the Year: 2006

DID YOU KNOW?

● Carles won a silver medal representing Spain at the 2000 Olympics in Sydney.
● He has a get-out clause in his contract that includes a £110m transfer fee!

PROFILE

THE BEAST OF Barcelona, Carles Puyol is the rock upon which the Catalan club's irresistible pool of attacking talent can build. The likes of Ronaldinho, Lionel Messi and Thierry Henry can all bomb forward and take risks on the ball, safe in the knowledge that Puyol is behind them, marshalling the Barca defence.

With his caveman appearance and intimidating physical presence, Puyol stands tall at the heart of Barcelona's defence, always willing to put his feet and head in where it hurts. Carles has been at the Nou Camp for his entire career and now established as club captain he seems set to end his career there.

Formerly a right-back, Carles has confirmed his status as a dominating centre-back in recent years. Impressive in the air but strongest on the deck, Puyol also has a good turn of pace and calmness on the ball. His desire and commitment inspire those around him to perform to their maximum.

Carles also skippers Spain's national side and helps bind together a young defence with his experience and organisational ability.

Certainly a defender you wouldn't want to mess with, Puyol is one of the most uncompromising around – just think of him as a Spanish John Terry with big hair!

WHAT HE SAYS

"This is FC Barcelona and sometimes you face criticism, but these things happen. We have to keep out of it and be stronger than ever, stick together, and among the squad, that is what we are doing."

SHOOTY SAYS:

He may have girl's hair but you wouldn't tell him that to his face! Puyol is a real rash of a defender who plays like an angry bull chasing a matador.

WILLY SAGNOL

ground down the flanks, offering a genuine attacking threat.

Willy has played for Bayern Munich since 2000 and has enhanced his reputation as an excellent man-marker and tough-tackling full-back at one of Europe's biggest clubs.

At the end of his first full season at Munich, Sagnol had helped his side clinch the Champions League and Bundesliga crowns.

Able to play as a wing-back or in midfield, Sagnol offers deadly accuracy with his delivery into the box from wide areas.

Has more than 50 caps for France but only really established himself as Les Blues' first choice right-back in 2004 when the great Marcel Desailly retired from international football and Lilian Thuram moved from right-back into central-defence.

FACTFILE

Full name: William Sagnol
Born: March 18, 1977,
Saint Etienne, France
Height: 1.8m (5ft 11in)
Weight: 78kg (12st 4lb)
Position: Right-back, right wing-back
Clubs: AS Saint-Etienne, AS Monaco and Bayern Munich

HONOURS

UEFA Champions League: 2001
Bundesliga: 2001, 2003, 2005, 2006
German Cup: 2003, 2005, 2006
Intercontinental Cup: 2001
Ligue One: 2000
Trophée des champions: 1997, 2000

DID YOU KNOW?

● Willy started every one of France's seven games as they reached the 2006 World Cup Final.
● Despite being one of the brightest performers on the pitch, Willy admits that he hates getting out of bed at the crack of dawn and dislikes body-punishing early morning training sessions!

PROFILE

THE FRANCE STAR is a pure athlete and one of the most consistent full-backs in European football. Sagnol is sound defensively and able to cover plenty of

WHAT HE SAYS

"I want to end my career in Bayern. Staying here is the best thing for my career. I've been in Munich for seven years and I don't want to change countries again."

SHOOTY SAYS:

A solid performer for club and country, Sagnol is currently one of the best right-backs in Europe. This Willy has proved he isn't a wonka.

WILLY SAGNOL

JOHN
TERRY

JOHN TERRY

FACTFILE

Full name: John George Terry
Born: December 7, 1980,
Barking, Essex
Height: 1.85m (6ft 1in)
Weight: 91.1kg (14st 5lb)
Position: Central-defender
Clubs: Nottingham Forest (loan)
and Chelsea

HONOURS

Premier League: 2005, 2006
FA Cup: 2000, 2007
League Cup: 2005, 2007

DID YOU KNOW?

● John became the first Chelsea
skipper in 50 years to lift the
English league title when the Blues
were crowned champions in 2005.
● He married long-time girlfriend Toni Poole
in June 2007. The couple, who live in the posh
Oxshott area of Surrey surrounded by other
Chelsea players, have twins, a boy and a girl.

PROFILE

AN INFLUENTIAL LEADER for both club and country,
JT is one of the toughest and most uncompromising
defenders in Europe.

His displays for Chelsea have been one of the major
reasons for the club's impressive league form in recent
seasons, and alongside Ricardo Carvalho in the centre
of defence, he has formed an awesome foundation for
the attacking players to build on.

John is commanding in the air and unflinching
in the tackle and his bravery when boots are flying
in is legendary. He also offers a genuine goalscoring
threat at corners and free-kicks and has a pretty
good range of passing.

He is a true lion heart for England, leading by
example and often defying medical logic to recover
from injuries that would leave others
sidelined for weeks.

John made his Chelsea debut in 1998
and became club captain in 2004. His
England bow came against Serbia and
Montenegro in 2003 and he was named
as David Beckham's successor as
international skipper in 2006.

WHAT HE SAYS

"I am so superstitious. I've got to have
the same seat on the bus, tie the tapes
around my socks three times and cut my tubular
grips for my shin-pads the same size every
game. I drive to games listening to the same
Usher CD in my car. It's good music to get me
pumped up and relaxed at the same time."

SHOOTY SAYS:

JT is England's and
Chelsea's bionic man
and defo one of the top
defenders in Europe!
Don't mess with him or
he'll break you in two!

KOLO TOURE

defence to start attacks. Has improved his concentration and decision-making and is well on his way to becoming the Gunners' next great centre-back following in the footsteps of Tony Adams and Sol Campbell.

Often captains Arsenal and despite his relatively young age of 26, he is one of the most experienced and senior members of Arsene Wenger's young side. The speedy centre-back, who cost just £150,000, is a regular for his country and well on his way to earning more than 50 caps.

FACTFILE

Full name: Kolo Habib Toure
Born: 19 March, 1981, Sokoura Bouake, Ivory Coast
Height: 1.83m (6ft)
Weight: 76kg (12st)
Position: Central-defender
Clubs: ASEC Mimosas and Arsenal

HONOURS

Premier League: 2004
FA Cup: 2003, 2005

DID YOU KNOW?

● Kolo's younger brother Yaya plays in midfield for Spanish giants Barcelona.
● He played in all five games for the Ivory Coast as they finished runners-up to the hosts in the African Cup of Nations in Egypt in January 2006.

PROFILE

KOLO TOURE SEEMS to get better as the seasons go by. He is now regarded as one of the most consistent defenders in the Premiership and an important player in the multi-talented and multi-cultural Arsenal team.

The Ivory Coast star has strength, pace and a great spring when jumping for headers, and is also comfortable on the ball and able to bring it out of

WHAT HE SAYS

"I can see myself staying at Arsenal for the rest of my career. Why would I want to leave? I love my football here, my family is settled here and the club is ambitious. It is fantastic. I always try to do my best for them. I love to give everything I have for people who come to see us - the people who have been working hard all week and pay their money to watch us. You have to do it for them. That is what is important."

SHOOTY SAYS:

Kolo is a great example of what makes a great modern defender. He has pace, strength and a fair bit of skill. Toure is tops!

KOLO
TOURE

NEMANJA VIDIC

NEMANJA VIDIC

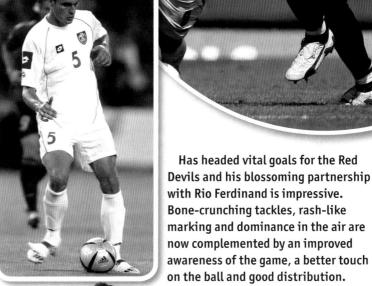

FACTFILE

Full name: Nemanja Vidic
Born: October 21, 1981,
Titovo Uzice, Yugoslavia
Height: 1.85m (6ft 1in)
Weight: 82.5kg (13st)
Position: Central-defender
Clubs: Red Star Belgrade, Spartak
Subotica (loan), Spartak Moscow
and Manchester United.

HONOURS

Premier League: 2007
League Cup: 2006
Serbian Superliga: 2004
Yugoslav Cup: 2002
Serbia and Montenegro Cup: 2004

DID YOU KNOW?

● Vidic was part of the Serbia and Montenegro national team's "Famous Four" defence that conceded just one goal during the side's ten 2006 FIFA World Cup qualification matches – the best record of any of the qualifying teams.
● Nemanja missed out on all of his country's three World Cup matches during the 2006 tournament. He was suspended for the first fixture against Holland and suffered a knee injury in training that ruled him out of the rest.

PROFILE

THE THOUGHT OF Nemanja Vidic challenging for a tackle or a header makes most centre-forwards wince. During his short spell in England, Nemanja has earned legendary status with Man United fans.

The Serbian took a few months to settle in the Premiership following his big money move from Spartak Moscow, but is now fully adjusted to the pace and style of the top-flight and with a winner's medal in his back pocket, Vidic is proving one of the best defenders in the division.

Has headed vital goals for the Red Devils and his blossoming partnership with Rio Ferdinand is impressive. Bone-crunching tackles, rash-like marking and dominance in the air are now complemented by an improved awareness of the game, a better touch on the ball and good distribution.

WHAT HE SAYS

"The start was hard for me. I arrived having not trained for 40 days because in Russia the season was finished. Injuries caused problems for me - these were hard days and months. But I learned so much. Every day, in every training session, at every moment, Sir Alex gives more than just advice."

SHOOTY SAYS:

Rumour has it that he turned up late for training once so Fergie fined the rest of the team for being early! The Serbinator is not to be messed with!

GIANLUCA ZAMBROTTA

FACTFILE

Full name: Gianluca Zambrotta
Born: February 19, 1977, Como, Italy.
Height: 1.8m (5ft 11in)
Weight: 76kg (12st)
Position: Full-back
Clubs: Como, AS Bari, Juventus and Barcelona

HONOURS

World Cup: 2006
Serie A: 2002, 2003, 2005, 2006 (2005 and 2006 titles stripped due to corruption and financial irregularities involving Juventus)
Supercoppa Italiana: 2002, 2003

DID YOU KNOW?

● Zambrotta mostly played as a winger until current Italy coach Marcello Lippi converted him into a left-back whilst the pair were both at Juventus.
● Gianluca represented the Italian team at the 2000 Sydney Olympics.

PROFILE

ZAMBROTTA IS WIDELY regarded as one of the finest attacking full-backs in Europe. He is a naturally talented defender but also has pace and skill to get forward and set attacks in motion. The Italian's amazing energy levels and ability to cover ground ensure he can also operate in a wing-back role.

Gianluca can also play in midfield and enjoyed success further up the pitch whilst on the books at Juventus. He is two-footed and comfortable defending from either flank, using his strength and ability in the air to dominate attackers.

Zambrotta played a major part in Italy's 2006 World Cup success, as he and left-full back Fabio Grosso bombed forward to supplement the attack, often making the extra man.

Now with Barcelona, Gianluca's ability on the ball has improved and his passing and delivery into the box are always deadly accurate. His experience and steely determination will be vital to Barca in La Liga and the Champions League.

WHAT HE SAYS

"I've played on the left with Juventus and on the right for the national team. It is really up to the coach to decide where he wants to play me. I'm not worried. I can play both positions equally well."

SHOOTY SAYS:

This Italian stallion really means business when he crosses the white line. Determined, focused and skilful on the ball, Zam the man is top class!

GIANLUCA
ZAMBROTTA

Nearly made it!

SHAY GIVEN

FACTFILE

Full name: Seamus John James Given
Born: April 20, 1976, Lifford, County Donegal
Height: 1.85m (6ft 1in)
Weight: 84.4kg (13st 4lb)
Position: Goalkeeper

DID YOU KNOW?

● Shay equalled Packie Bonner's record for most Republic of Ireland caps won by a keeper when he hit 80 appearances in March 2007.
● The shot-stopper has turned out more than 420 times for the Magpies and by the end of season 2007-08 should be in their top four appearance-makers of all time.

WHY DID HE MISS THE LIST?

Somebody has to be the first person to miss out on the prizes and Shay can count himself unlucky not to hit the Top 20. He'd be first-choice for virtually ever Premier League team when fit. He's not the tallest keeper around but he makes up for that with his agility and in recent years has improved his kicking ability which was probably his only major fault.

GARY NEVILLE

FACTFILE

Full name: Gary Alexander Neville
Born: February 18, 1975, Bury, Greater Manchester
Height: 1.78m (5ft 10in)
Weight: 72.1kg (11st 5lb)
Position: Right-back, centre-half

DID YOU KNOW?

● Already England's most-capped right-back, when Gary reaches 86 appearances for his country he will equal the Three Lions' all-time best for a full-back.
● In nearly 16 years with United he's made more than 500 appearances, winning seven Premiership titles, three FA Cups, a European Cup and one League Cup.

WHY DID HE MISS THE LIST?

If it hadn't been for his age, the Man United legend would probably have made the final list. Having missed most of 2007 through injury, he slipped down the rankings a little. Although he's not popular with supporters of clubs other than United, his determination in an England shirt cannot be faulted.

MICAH RICHARDS

FACTFILE

Full name: Micah Lincoln Richards
Born: June 24, 1988, Birmingham
Height: 1.8m (5ft 11in)
Weight: 86kg (13st 8lb)
Position: Right-back, central-defender

DID YOU KNOW?

● Micah has been capped at Under-16, 19 and 21 levels for England and became the country's youngest-ever defender when he pulled on a senior shirt in November 2006.

● Born in Birmingham, raised in Leeds, Micah began his career as a schoolboy at Oldham, but admits Arsenal are the team he used to support!

WHY DID HE MISS THE LIST?

Micah is definitely one for the future. But having only made his Man City debut in October 2005 and first England start in November 2006, he's got quite a way to go to reach the very top. His skill, strength, speed, reading of the game and sheer determination should mean it won't be long before he's rated world-class.

Here are six top-class defenders and a keeper who can count themselves unlucky not to make our final list...

LEDLEY KING

FACTFILE
Full name: Ledley Brenton King
Born: October 12, 1980, Bow, East London
Height: 1.88m (6ft 2in)
Weight: 86kg (13st 8lb)
Position: Central-defence, defensive midfielder

DID YOU KNOW?
● Ledley had to leave Euro 2004 in Portugal early when his girlfriend went into labour with their baby. He watched the quarter-final game back home in England.
● He was the player who stepped into Sol Campbell's boots when the central-defender left for big rivals Arsenal. Ledley later played alongside his hero for England.

WHY DID HE MISS THE LIST?
The Tottenham captain's ability cannot be faulted and although he's first and foremost a centre-half, he has proved for both club and country that he is also at home playing just in front of the back line. His biggest problem recently has been a series of injuries.

PAOLO MALDINI

FACTFILE
Full name: Paolo Maldini
Born: June 26, 1968, Milan, Italy
Height: 1.86m (6ft 1in)
Weight: 83kg (13st 1lb)
Position: Central-defender, left-back

DID YOU KNOW?
● His list of silverware includes seven Serie A titles, five Italian Cups, five European Cups, five European Super Cups – and that's just the major stuff!
● Paolo's teenage son plays for Milan's junior side. You wouldn't want to be following in this Dad's footsteps!

WHY DID HE MISS THE LIST?
Approaching his 40th birthday, Paolo is obviously well past his sell-by date, but being sold is something that's never happened to him... he's been with AC Milan all his career, a staggering 24 years! Quite simply, he's superb and that's why we had to give him a mention. A few years ago nobody would have argued about him being No.1 on the list.

GABRIEL HEINZE

FACTFILE
Full name: Gabriel Ivan Heinze
Born: March 19, 1978, Crespo, Argentina
Height: 1.78m (5ft 10in)
Weight: 78kg (12st 4lb)
Position: Left-back, centre-back

DID YOU KNOW?
● Gabby was Man United fans' Player of the Year in 2005, pipping top scorer Wayne Rooney to the award.
● He agreed a four-year deal with Real Madrid after a £8m move from Old Trafford in summer 2007.

WHY DID HE MISS THE LIST?
A regular for Argentina, and a hero during his days at United due to his crunching tackles and creative runs forward, Heinze fell out with Fergie when the Old Trafford boss blocked a move to rivals Liverpool. Once you get on the wrong side of Fergie your United days are numbered! Injuries restricted his chances of making an early mark at the Bernabeu but once he gets a run of games for Real Madrid, expect him to challenge our Top 20.